Original title:
Cosmic Cowpies

Copyright © 2025 Creative Arts Management OÜ
All rights reserved.

Author: Levi Montgomery
ISBN HARDBACK: 978-1-80567-793-2
ISBN PAPERBACK: 978-1-80567-914-1

Celestial Cow Cud

In the sky, the cows do graze,
Chewing stars in a cosmic haze.
They drop their treats with playful cheer,
As stardust sparkles, drawing near.

Galactic glee from clouds they bring,
With each plop, the universe sings.
Mooing laughter fills the night,
As space-donuts take their flight.

Starlight Soil

From distant fields of twinkling light,
Comes soil that glows, oh what a sight!
With every scoop, a giggle so bright,
As alien plants dance in delight.

Worms in orbit do a wiggly twist,
Creating laughter in the cosmic mist.
Each sprinkle of dirt brings a funny scene,
Where buttercups bloom in shades of green.

Ethereal Excrement

A comet's tail, a spacey gift,
In zero-gravity, watch it lift!
Floating chunks with a giggly flair,
Turn the vacuum into a fair.

Planets chuckle as they collide,
With jolly beams of joy and pride.
Astronauts brush off their starry shoes,
As they tip their hats to this cosmic muse.

Cosmic Currents

Waves of laughter ripple and sway,
In skies where interstellar cows play.
Riding the currents, they frolic with glee,
Leaving tracks of giggles 'cross the galaxy.

Fleeting moments of farcical grace,
As laughter echoes through time and space.
With every moo, the cosmos ignites,
A funny dance in the starry nights.

Infinite Fertility

In the fields where stardust grows,
Galactic greens in rows and rows.
Each puff of wind brings forth a laugh,
As space-goats munch on cosmic chaff.

From planets round and moons so bright,
They churn out treats by day and night.
With every hop, a gleeful leap,
They leave behind a treasure heap.

Astral Adornments

Glittering gems from skies above,
Are scattered gifts from interstellar love.
A wink from Venus, a nod from Mars,
Crafts a charm that's full of stars.

Shiny spheres that gently roll,
Each one a story, a spacey goal.
With giggles echoing through the void,
These playful stars leave us overjoyed.

Cosmic Crumbs

As comets fly and meteors dash,
They leave behind a gentle splash.
A sprinkle here, a glimmer there,
The universe loves to share its fare.

Floating bits from realms afar,
Like breadcrumbs from a giant's jar.
Gathered by the curious throng,
Laughing as they hum a tune so strong.

Twinkling Turds

In the vast expanse where giggles bloom,
There lies a sight that chases gloom.
Sprightly bits that twinkle bright,
A silly jest in the starry night.

With chuckles shared among the stars,
Rolling by in space-bound cars.
What joy it brings, that wondrous sight,
Of twinkling mischief that feels so right!

Moonbeam Muck

Up in the sky where the laughter flies,
Moonbeams dance with silly surprise.
They trip on tales of stardust farts,
Dropping giggles that fill our hearts.

Crusty comets with cookie crumbs,
Leave trails of chuckles and silly sums.
A bunny leaps through a lunar loop,
Wobbling in the galactic troop.

Quasarian Quagmire

In a swirl of stars, the giggles grow,
A barnyard dance in a cosmic show.
Wobbling pigs on a trampoline,
Bouncing high in a stellar scene.

Space cows moo in a twinkling tune,
Juggling meteors beneath the moon.
They slip and slide in the asteroid's grip,
On rubbery feet, they waddle and skip.

Gravity's Grains

A grain of sand in an endless loop,
Wobbling like a clumsy troop.
It floats on beams of cosmic cheer,
Tickling toes of the creatures near.

Starry snacks and silly spills,
Platinum pancakes give us thrills.
We flip and flop in a stellar race,
Laughing hard in this weightless space.

Spacetime Spoilage

In a blender made of swirling light,
Soupy stars applause in the night.
A cherry comet takes a wrong turn,
Splashing sauce where the planets churn.

Jelly jars float in the vacuum's kiss,
Bringing sandwiches we can't resist.
With every bite, the laughter soars,
As we munch on space-time leftovers galore!

Cosmic Clusters

In the galaxy's field, things float and swirl,
There are strange little bits that make us twirl.
Stars shine bright, while whispers giggle,
Over space's snacks, they dance and wiggle.

Planets watch from afar with delight,
As the universe plays hide and seek at night.
Each glimmering speck, a comical sight,
Reminds us that space is full of light.

Meteor Manure

Shooting stars dash with a rosy flare,
But behind them trails what they no longer care.
Galactic leftovers, a fragrant plume,
Leaving footprints of laughter across the gloom.

The Milky Way winks as it passes by,
Sprinkling space dust and a sly alibi.
What's golden in hue is nature's best blunder,
And under its glow, we can't help but wonder!

Supernova Soil

From the cradle of chaos, a garden blooms,
With cosmic crumbs and colorful fumes.
Nature chuckles at the wonders of fate,
Where aliens giggle and planets play straight.

Comets whisk by with playful grace,
Creating a soil that's a starry embrace.
It tickles the roots of astrological trees,
As laughter grows wild, swaying with ease.

Celestial Splatters

Look at the sky, a canvas of fun,
With blobs of color as the day is done.
Mars drips red as Jupiter grins,
While Saturn spins tales of cosmic wins.

Each splash tells a story, absurd and bright,
Of a universe bursting with infinite light.
And in this mayhem, we giggle and sway,
For everywhere thoughts of space play!

Cosmic Composts

In a galaxy far, far away,
Moo-ing creatures dance and play,
Beneath the stars, they scatter their dung,
A squishy treat for the sprouts so young.

Compost heaps full of wiggling worms,
Beneath the moons, strange lifeforms squirm,
With a gentle breeze, the scent just wafts,
Galactic gardening—what a good laugh!

Starship Stability

On a ship that flies past Mars,
An engineer drops his snacks from jars,
But oh, the giggles and the chuckles,
When everyone slips on the cosmic chuckles.

Wobbling through space, all hands on deck,
Avoiding the slides—oh, what the heck!
With some gooey bits stuck to their boots,
They navigate orbits in silly suits!

Supernova Spoils

When superstars burst into the night,
They leave behind a comical sight,
With glowing globs that look like treats,
Silly smears of space-time feats.

Aliens gather, their laughter aligns,
As they scoop up the gooey designs,
With buckets and spoons, they slurp up the fun,
Creating a mess when the day is done!

Celestial Calves

In a field of stars, the cattle roam,
With twinkling tails, they feel at home,
As they chew on the milky way grass,
They giggle and moo at all that has passed.

These lunar calves have a right ol' time,
Jumping through comets, oh, isn't it sublime?
Starlight blinks as they leap in glee,
Creating a splash wherever they be!

Celestial Compost

From stardust droppings, smiles arise,
Planets chuckle beneath the skies.
Galactic gardens, full of glee,
Nurtured by what once was free.

Aliens dance in cosmic plays,
While laughter echoes through the bays.
Sprinkling joy on moons so bright,
In this realm, there's pure delight.

Intergalactic Ingestion

Spaceships feast on floating pies,
Nibbling on treats that swim and fly.
Gravity's buffet, a sight to see,
They munch and crunch with giddy glee.

Comets whip up a tasty stew,
Slurping sounds from a crew so true.
Yummy bites from afar they take,
With every chew, they giggle and shake.

Meteorite Muff

Baking muffins from moonlit dust,
A recipe that's a bit of a must.
Lunar lumps and solar spice,
Each bite is silly, oh so nice!

Asteroids in a pastry whirl,
Doughnuts from comets start to twirl.
They rise and puff in starry heat,
A cosmic treat that's hard to beat.

Nebulous Nurturance

In a cloud of giggles, seeds are sown,
Laughter grows in colors unknown.
Galaxies beam with joyful rays,
Recycling cheer in brilliant ways.

Planets hum tunes of natural fun,
While suns chase shadows till the day is done.
With quirky roots in bizarre terrain,
They sprout and dance, unchained by grain.

Nebula Nuggets

In the depths of space, a treasure lies,
Tiny bits of laughter that can mesmerize.
Floating through the stars, they twinkle bright,
Making even black holes giggle with delight.

A cosmic giggle, a playful tease,
Stardust giggles dance with the solar breeze.
With comet tails that tug at your heart,
These nuggets of joy, a celestial art.

Planets chuckle and twirl in glee,
As they pass these gems, joyful as can be.
In the vast cosmic scheme, oh what a sight,
To find little nuggets that sparkle at night.

Astral Excrement

On a starlit night, what could that be?
A sparkle so cheeky, just for you and me.
Asteroids giggle, as they roll on past,
Leaving trails of laughter, a humor that lasts.

In the vastness of void, a prankster's delight,
Droplets of joy dance in the pale light.
They twirl through the cosmos, a glittery spree,
Making meteors chuckle in unison with glee.

Galaxies chuckle, bursting with cheer,
As comets race by in a cosmic veneer.
Is it art, or just playful refuse?
In the universe, anything's fair game to use!

Radiant Residue

In the spiral arms of the Milky Way's hug,
Residue sparkles like a shiny bug.
Galactic giggles echo from afar,
As light-years of laughter dance like a star.

Floating through time where the jokes are deep,
Bright remnants of fun make the cosmos leap.
Messy and wild, like a comet's bold tail,
In the realm of the stars, humor will prevail.

Saintly stardust from a cosmic kite,
Painting the night with mischievous light.
With a sprinkle of joy that just won't quit,
This radiant residue is pure comedic wit!

Planets' Poop

Round and round they go, in orbital glee,
Planets play games, oh, what a spree!
With each little spin, they share a sly grin,
Dropping little treasures that make us all win.

Saturn's rings laugh, oh what a show!
Laughter from Jupiter takes us with a flow.
Pluto chimes in with a wink of the eye,
Sending out chuckles as he floats by.

It's a playful dance, a cosmic affair,
Filled with guffaws that float everywhere.
From the sun's warm rays to the dark cosmic sweep,
Their silly little gifts give us joy in our sleep.

Universal Field Offerings

In the fields where stardust grows,
Strange offerings from space, who knows?
A comet's twist, a planet's waddle,
Seems like they just love to dawdle.

Jupiter's rings, a sparkly lace,
Sprinkled 'round this silly place.
Asteroids roll on without care,
Leaving behind their playful fare.

Galaxies laugh in their mighty dance,
Flinging moon pies with a comical chance.
Silly creatures on the ground,
Giggling at what they have found.

With each bounce, a joyful sound,
Gifts from the skies come tumbling down.
In this space, so vast and bright,
Laughter echoes through the night.

Cosmic Fertility

In fields where stars and planets play,
Life sprouts in a most humorous way.
Comets drop their shiny seeds,
Growing laughter like wild weeds.

Underneath the lunar light,
Critters dance with pure delight.
Mars sends blooms of feathery dust,
As the walkers waddle, it's a must.

Moons spin tales of wobbly sprout,
While meteors laugh and spin about.
In this garden, a cosmic jest,
Every leaf a laughter quest.

So join the fun, don't miss the chance,
To twirl with joy in a cosmic dance.
Fertile ground of galactic fun,
Where jokes are birthed and laughter's spun.

Milky Way Mulch

In gardens where the stars align,
Milky splotches add a shine.
From twinkling dust, we do create,
A mulch of chuckles, oh so great.

Interstellar mix of giggles and glee,
Growing wonders for all to see.
From each zany plot, a story's spun,
While space critters laugh and run.

Gravel paths with starlight streaks,
Fill the universe with playful peaks.
Comets chat while asteroids play,
In the garden of the Milky Way.

Plant your heart in this joyful realm,
Let laughter and stardust overwhelm.
With every sprinkle of silly stuff,
Milky Way mulch is more than enough.

Galactic Grazing Grounds

In the pastures of twinkling rhyme,
Grazing beasts of space take their time.
Nibbling on photons, munching on light,
They frolic through the galactic night.

Starry herds in a cosmic spree,
Chasing rainbows, wild and free.
With a burp, they send out surprises,
As laughter echoes 'neath bright skies.

Supernova pies placed on high,
Galactic munching, oh my, oh my!
With each silly snack, they emit a chuckle,
While cosmic winds playfully shuffle.

Galactic grounds, a buffet of fun,
With each playful bite, the day is won.
So join the feast, don't hesitate,
In this space of laughter, don't be late!

Galactic Goodies

In the dark of space, so wide and vast,
Droppings float by, they sure move fast.
Little brown blobs with a twinkling glow,
Chasing them feels like a cosmic show.

Aliens giggle as they take a scoop,
Making sweet treats for their merry group.
Flavor of stardust, a sprinkle of cheer,
Snack time in space, things couldn't be clear.

With laughter echoing through the whole void,
These odd little morsels we can't avoid.
For every cow pie that zips right by,
Anecdotes ripple, no need to be shy!

So when you launch to that great unknown,
Keep an eye out for the treats they've shown.
Floating delights in a spat of delight,
Galactic goodies are sure outta sight!

Celestial Cow Plops

In the nebula where the rockets zoom,
Majestic cows drift in cosmic gloom.
With bells a-jingling, they take a turn,
Dropping their treasures, a sight to discern.

Each plop a comet, what a wild ride,
Sprinkling stardust on the galactic tide.
Astronauts giggle in their suits so tight,
Dancing through space till the morning light.

Hovering close to a mooing star,
They swirl in laughter, wishing on a czar.
For every big splat that crashes down,
A new recipe forms for the space-faring clown!

So next time you gaze at the Milky Way,
Think of the laughter these gaggles convey.
A whimsical world, full of cow pie dreams,
Where space is just funny, or so it seems!

Astronaut's Aftermath

Suit on snug, they launch with a grin,
To the stars beyond, let the fun begin.
But oh what a mess, from the lunch they dine,
Cleverly wrapped in this vacuum design!

Floating behind, with a wiggly bounce,
The leftovers dance, they jiggle and flounce.
Did they pack snacks or are those true blues?
Full of mystery, a cosmic refuse.

With giggles and hiccups, they share the tale,
Of galactic remnants that start to trail.
As space cows chuckle, they join in the jest,
Making the void feel like home at best.

So astronauts laugh at the chaos untamed,
Each mishap a memory, never the same.
In the grand void, there's a trickster's art,
Floating through space, with a light, funny heart!

Starlit Scatology

Under the stars, in the vast expanse,
Strange little droppings begin to dance.
Astronomy books never prepared us for this,
Nature's odd gifts, all wrapped in bliss.

Planets adorned in whimsical flair,
With peculiar plops floating everywhere.
Rocketmen chuckle, it's all but a game,
In this weird universe, it's all the same.

Stardust dust bunnies spin through the night,
Causing collide with a comical fright.
Who knew the cosmos could be so absurd?
With laughter and joy, their beauty's ensured.

So cheer for the humor in interstellar scats,
From squishy surprises to stellar spats.
In this delightful dance, we find constant glee,
With each little plop lighting up the spree!

Cosmic Cultivation

In fields of stars, we till the ground,
With jokers laughing, what a sound.
Galactic grins, we plant and play,
Harvesting giggles, every day.

Martian mud, it's quite a scene,
Alien crops, a vibrant green.
Silly plants with squiggly tops,
Under the sun, the laughter never stops.

In space, we grow our wacky dreams,
With astro-fertilizer, nothing's as it seems.
Cosmic carrots and moonlight beans,
Dancing veggies in cosmic streams.

So come aboard this playful ride,
Where whimsy blooms, and joy won't hide.
With laughter rising to the stars,
Each harvest brings new clownish jars.

Stratospheric Slop

In the clouds, a slushy mess,
Space-faring chefs, they do their best.
Mixing flavors from beyond the light,
Slurping up joy, oh what a sight!

Galactic goo in a big bowl,
Floating flavors take their toll.
Slappy space pies, so hard to resist,
A splat of giggles is on the list.

Zero-gravity, slop goes wide,
Bouncing bites, what a wild ride!
With every spoonful, laughter flows,
In this airborne feast, anything goes.

So grab your forks and take a chance,
Join the fun, and join the dance.
Stratospheric splatter across the sky,
In this tasty chaos, let laughter fly!

Stellar Spoils

Beneath the stars, we gather round,
With silly treasure to be found.
Stellar spoils, a quirky sight,
Laughter echoes, shining bright.

Galaxies filled with jiggly treats,
Alien sweets that bounce on feet.
Fizzy orbs and rainbow pies,
Momentary joy that never dies.

In a nebula of silly fun,
Giggling under a bouncy sun.
Treasure maps made of jelly beans,
Each step taken bursts at the seams.

So come together, take the leap,
In this vast universe, let's not weep.
For in the spoils of laughter's light,
Every moment's pure delight!

Heavenly Handouts

Up in the skies, a surprise affair,
With heavenly handouts floating in air.
A sprinkle of joy, a dash of fun,
    Sassy snacks for everyone!

Cosmic cookies from a starry tray,
Whimsical wonders, come out to play.
Galaxy gumdrops, on each plate,
    Giggling groups cannot wait.

Bubbly drinks served in scoops,
Mapped out laughter with silly loops.
Jovial treats for those who seek,
In this feast, we all can speak.

So take a seat on this glowing craft,
Share some giggles and a good laugh.
With heavenly gifts from the skies above,
We celebrate together, all in love!

Astronomical Artifacts

In the sky, a shimmering sight,
Strange shapes dance in the night.
Glittering chunks, a celestial mess,
Floating around, what a funny dress!

Meteorites with a twist of fate,
Some look like cheese, isn't that great?
Collecting these gems from afar,
Is like chasing dreams on a shooting star.

Orbital Offerings

Planets serve a quirky feast,
From gassy burgers to starlit yeast.
Galactic treats, oh what a sight,
Nibbling comets, a true delight!

Saturn's rings are a circus show,
Juggling moons — oh, how they glow!
Each bite a journey, a cosmic race,
Dining in space, what a wild place!

Cosmic Windfall

Stardust falling like confetti bright,
Tickling noses in the dead of night.
Galaxies laughing with a twinkling grin,
What a riot beneath this stellar spin!

Asteroids rolling like bowling balls,
Hitting planets, oh what a call!
Each crash a joke in the cosmic play,
As laughter echoes, floating away.

Interstellar Ingredients

A pinch of stardust, a dash of light,
Cooking with comets feels just right.
Mixing black holes in a giant pot,
What's the recipe? I've forgot!

Galactic spoons and nebula knives,
Whipping up meals that tickle lives.
Mars may serve the strangest stew,
But who can resist? It's fun to chew!

Celestial Crop

In the sky, a scatter of space,
A bovine dance with an alien grace.
With laughter echoing off the moons,
They leave behind their milky tunes.

Shooting stars with a curious smell,
Moonbeams giggle, they know it well.
The planets spin with a cheeky cheer,
As comet trails draw us near.

The nebulae wink, a mischievous sight,
As the cattle roam in the dead of night.
Their interstellar antics are bits of delight,
Leaving wonders that take to flight.

Floating fields of a galactic joke,
A tasty treat, not just for folks.
With every plop, our worries flee,
In this cosmic farm, we're all carefree.

Star Studded Spoilage

In the void where the stardust dwells,
Bovine buddies cast curious spells.
Spaceships passing can't help but stop,
To observe the comedy at the crop.

Galactic gusts play hide and seek,
Uncovering treasures that truly stink.
Asteroids laugh in their orbit's chase,
As the universe shares a smelly embrace.

Grinning meteors fall in a line,
Wishing they had better wine.
The swirling soup of unique delights,
Makes space travel filled with giggly sights.

When comets crash with a humorous boom,
Even black holes can't suck up the gloom.
In this laughter-filled cosmic dance,
We find joy in every glance.

Galactic Grain

In a field where the comets twirl,
Spaced-out cows give the stars a whirl.
Their nightly jaunts, a frolicsome spree,
Plant cosmic crops for you and me.

Asteroids munch on celestial hay,
As planets gossip at the end of the day.
They graze on sparkles, nibble on light,
Belly laughs echo through the night.

Twinkling wonders dance all around,
In this realm, good humor is found.
Grain from deep space can't be confined,
To the jesters of joy, we're all aligned.

Silly satellites spin with delight,
As bovine laughter ignites the night.
A harvest of giggles from way up high,
In this wondrous universe, we'll fly.

Universal Uproar

In the endless stretch of the twinkling expanse,
Bovines prance like they're in a dance.
They leave behind their heavenly marks,
Creating art that ignites the sparks.

Galaxies chuckle, it's hard to ignore,
At the mooing sounds from a black hole's door.
They spin with joy in the cosmic spree,
As laughter echoes like waves from the sea.

Nebulas burst with colorful styles,
While floating farms grow light with smiles.
Grinning stars take a moment to jest,
In this universe, we're all blessed.

A ruckus erupts across the expanse,
As cows frolic in a carefree dance.
Galactic fun never feels out of place,
We share this laughter in outer space.

Universal Unravelings

In the void where meteors fly,
There's space debris drifting by.
Aliens giggle, what a sight,
Sending junk into the night.

Stardust tangled in a heap,
Galactic secrets they can't keep.
Out in orbit, laughs abound,
With every wacky find they've found.

Black holes swallow all they see,
But refuse to eat their leafy tea.
Supernovas burst with cheer,
Showering laughter everywhere near.

So raise a toast to outer space,
Where nonsense holds a special place.
Among the stars, we can relate,
To every cosmic twist of fate.

Shimmering Shit

Floating freely in the void,
A shiny prize, oh what a joy!
Twinkling gems from astral waste,
Even stars have had their taste.

A comet's tail, so full of sheen,
Turns out to be a cosmic bean.
Laughter echoes through the night,
At the sight of glittering blight.

Galaxies spin in a dizzy dance,
As we scoop up every chance.
Who knew the skies held such fun?
With a wink, the universe spun.

So gather 'round for tales so bold,
Of the shiny treasures we behold.
In every speck, there's joy and jest,
In this vast space, we're truly blessed.

Cometary Castoffs

Tiny rocks from a cosmic fling,
Dancing in the void, what a thing!
They glide and swirl, a merry ballet,
Leaving behind their crumbs of clay.

With every pass, they chuckle bright,
Dropping gems and bits of light.
What a mess, but oh so proud,
Shimmers shining, attracting a crowd.

Asteroids play, as space cows moo,
In fields of starlight, they dream anew.
From outside worlds, they send their cheer,
Casting laughter upon us here.

So next time you gaze at the skies,
Remember these wanderers, oh so wise.
Each comet's trail, a trail of glee,
In the great expanse, pure jubilee!

Galactic Graze

Out beyond the Saturn rings,
Space cows munch on cosmic things.
Eating grass made of stardust light,
In the milky void, delight takes flight.

They moo in rhythms, oh-so-fine,
As nebulae build their space-time dine.
Galloping through wormholes bright,
These bovine wonders spark the night.

Every burp sends stars away,
Creating comets in a playful sway.
With each trot, they jiggle and bounce,
In laughter's realm, the cosmos pounce.

So when you look at the night so wide,
Think of the cows with their starry ride.
For in every corner of the universe vast,
Lurks a humor that's sure to last.

Comet's Contribution

A comet zooms with a wagging tail,
Dropping goodies like a silly snail.
Stardust sprinkles on planets below,
Gifting giggles in a celestial show.

What a sight, the milky way's delight,
Perplexing creatures dance in the night.
They catch the sparkles with a clumsy cheer,
As laughter echoes far and near.

Meteor showers bring a bizarre brew,
Giggles and grins, they stick like glue.
With every splash of a cosmic treat,
Space-folk chuckle, can't be beat!

When the stars play tricks, oh what a sight,
Floating fluff balls drifting in flight.
A laughter riot in the cosmic spree,
Joyful chaos, just let it be!

Dark Matter Dung

In shadows deep where the wonders lay,
Strange stuff rests, not far away.
Invisible piles that sparkle and glow,
Making aliens giggle, oh what a show!

Gravity's stinker, it twists and turns,
Around black holes, the laughter churns.
It's odd, it's wacky, a real space funk,
Creating bright joy from the stuff we thunk.

With every whiff of cosmic surprise,
Stargazers chuckle beneath starry skies.
Silly constructs of matter that's dark,
Bringing forth giggles with each little quark.

So embrace the jest, don't be so serious,
Life in the void can be quite delirious.
Celebrate the weird with all of your might,
For joy in the void is a hilarious sight!

Extraterrestrial Essence

A wibbly blob from a distant sphere,
Gooey delight that brings forth cheer.
Bouncing and jiggling with glee untold,
This alien treat is a sight to behold!

With flavors unknown to the human tongue,
Every bite is a song that's wildly sung.
It burbles and giggles, it flips and flops,
Creating a ruckus, the laughter never stops.

From planets where fun reigns supreme,
Extraterrestrial snacks, what a dream!
Biting into joy, they twirl around,
As the universe chuckles with a happy sound.

So gather the essence from worlds afar,
Bring a spoon, we'll feast beneath a star!
With every flavor, a cosmic jest,
Join the hilarity, it's simply the best!

Orbiting Organics

Around and around in a jovial dance,
These quirky bits love to take a chance.
They spin and twirl in a merry parade,
Creating a ruckus, a cosmic charade!

With squishy shapes and colors that pop,
They bounce with joy, they never stop!
These orbiting bits have come to play,
Frolicking freely, oh what a display!

In the garden of stars where fun takes flight,
Silly happenings light up the night.
Each playful swirl is a giggling sight,
They twinkle and tickle till morning light!

So join the dance, let your spirits soar,
With orbiting wonders, you'll never bore.
In the realm of laughter, where dreams collide,
Hilarity reigns as we joyfully glide!

Galactic Grazing Grounds

In a field where stars do shine,
Space cows munch on grass divine.
They chew the Milky Way with glee,
Leaving trails of cosmic debris.

Asteroids bounce like lost balloons,
While cows sing out their silly tunes.
Hooves make craters, not a care,
In their galaxy without a scare.

Planets roll like giant rocks,
As cows wear boots and cozy socks.
With every burp, a supernova,
Their joy is cosmic, like a sofa.

So watch out for those grassy patches,
Where laughter rings and joy dispatches.
In fields where laughter fills the night,
Cows of space can take their flight.

Moonlit Manure

Upon the hills where moonbeams glow,
Farmers chase down cattle's flow.
With every pile, a comet's tail,
The stench of space, a funny tale.

With a chuckle, they clean the ground,
Hopping 'round like they're spellbound.
The manure sparkles, shines and shines,
Turning into starry designs.

When night falls, they dance and play,
While the cows dream the night away.
Galactic jokes, they share with pride,
As planets giggle by their side.

Cows drift off in lunar sleep,
While twinkling lights are scattered deep.
Their moonlit leavings, a sight so grand,
Transforming worlds at their command.

Interstellar Pasture

Across the skies where comets race,
Cows graze in a funny place.
With space grass green and fresh to eat,
They frolic 'round with dancing feet.

Each moo sends ripples through the stars,
As cows bathe in light from Mars.
They stick their heads into the fray,
Nibbling on the Milky Way.

With smiles bright as quasars flash,
They leap around with a cosmic clash.
Every belch sends meteors flying,
In their world, there's no denying.

So join the fun, don't miss the ride,
Through pastures where the cows abide.
In this wild, whimsical terrain,
Laughing cattle drive the mundane.

Lunar Leavings

On silver hills where craters swell,
Cows slide down with a giggling yell.
Their lunar leavings, quite the sight,
    Glowing softly in the night.

With every leap, they start to twirl,
Leaving footprints in a wide swirl.
Their wondrous mess, a starry craft,
In space's playground, their joyful draft.

While astronauts sip their cosmic tea,
Cows frolic wild and feel so free.
With bells that jingle like a plan,
For laughter reigns wherever they ran.

So come and see this funny scene,
Where space is filled with joy serene.
In every cowpoke's happy dance,
There's magic in their starlit prance.

Celestial Composting

In the dark of the night, they float,
Little nuggets in a distant boat.
Stars giggle and twinkle with glee,
As they see spaceships take a spree.

Galactic gardeners in space so bright,
Planting laughs with all their might.
A dash of humor, a sprinkle of cheer,
Composting laughter, year after year.

Milky Way Manure

From the center of the galaxy, a whiff,
Of something strange—a cosmic tiff.
A comet sneezed, oh what a sight,
With laughter echoing all through the night.

Aliens chuckling, holding their noses,
As they dance with starry poses.
In the Milky Way, they take their chance,
To make the universe giggle and prance.

Universal Uplift

Planets spinning, what a scene!
Mixing humor with the unseen.
Laughter lifts the weight of space,
Creating joy in every place.

A celestial grin spreads afar,
With each belly laugh, they raise the bar.
Trading frowns for cosmic delight,
As the stardust sparkles bright.

Stellar Surplus

Flares and sparks in every corner,
The universe a playful mourner.
Sheepish meteors, they float and sway,
Creating chuckles in a rowdy play.

A surplus of joy from the skies above,
In every wink, there's laughter—love.
Twinkling comets dropping their jest,
In the vastness, they find their fest.

Lunar Lushness

On a moonlit field, they graze with glee,
Space cows munching on grass that's free.
With twinkling stars, they pick and chew,
    Filling the night with a bovine stew.

Galactic pastures, oh what a sight,
In the warm glow of the starry light.
Winking aliens join in the fun,
    Dancing around till the day is done.

With every stomp, they shake the ground,
    Creating laughter, oh such a sound!
They leap up high, then land with a thud,
    Leaving behind a sparkling mud.

So if you gaze at the night sky's art,
Remember the cows that play a part.
Their joyful antics, a comical spree,
    In a universe filled with glee.

Cosmic Critter Contributions

In a field of stars, cows play in the night,
Belly-laughing and munching with delight.
They leave behind treasures, a stinky surprise,
Sparkling gems that asteroids prize.

Each critter's job is cosmic and grand,
Dropping their pearls across the land.
Some giggle and moo, what a silly crew,
Creating confetti where they once blew.

Asteroids roll, thinking they're wise,
While cows toss stardust and playful pies.
With every jump, a meteorite,
Becomes the backdrop of their silly flight.

Oh, the universe laughs at their spree,
As cosmic critters frolic, wild and free.
Nature's prankster, turning dark to bright,
With each silly step, they make it just right.

Astral Enrichment

From a distant star, a curious moo,
Echoes through space, searching for stew.
Grab a comet tail for a salad delight,
Their unique recipes make dinner take flight.

In the garden of galaxies, cows dance with flair,
Twirling on orbits, with not a care.
With a flip of a tail, they snag a star,
Befriending the planets, both near and far.

Lunar ketchup drizzled from above,
Brings laughter and warmth, like a hug of love.
They campaign for taste, with giggles and glee,
Turning each moment into a jubilee.

So join this feast, in the vastness so wide,
Where laughter and chaos joyfully collide.
Astral enrichment, a zany affair,
With cows of the cosmos, dancing in air.

Heavenly Herds

In the sky's wide expanse, cows float on by,
With wings made of dreams, they soar up high.
They munch on moonbeams and giggle in delight,
Painting the heavens in sparkles so bright.

The herds play hopscotch on Saturn's rings,
Making music that twirls and sings.
With every leap, there's laughter and cheer,
Creating a ruckus for all to hear.

With bubbles of laughter, they drift and sway,
Chasing the comets that zip past their way.
Each cosmic jump brings a new point of view,
Under the stars they frolic anew.

So look to the skies when night comes around,
For heavenly herds that frolic abound.
With a chuckle and moo, they light up the night,
In a universe filled with sheer delight.

Solar Silage

In fields of sun, where laughter grows,
The crops are bright with cosmic prose.
A tractor's dance in swirling light,
Harvesting smiles, what pure delight!

With every turn, the stars align,
As veggies twirl, they sip on wine.
A moonbeam freshens every leaf,
While giggles echo, sweet relief!

Galactic barns and shooting stars,
Where veggies wear their camouflage.
They prance and bounce to playful beats,
In milky ways of veggie feats!

Oh, let us toast with sparkling cheer,
To leafy greens and cosmic beer.
For in this field of funny dreams,
Life bursts forth in solar beams!

Intergalactic Irrigation

Rain from above, a splashy sight,
Sprinklers dance in pure delight.
Watering plants with wacky tunes,
As aliens clap under the moons.

Cosmic hoses twist and twine,
They sing and rotate, oh so fine.
Galaxies spin, and laughter flows,
While droplets sparkle like glowing shows!

Down the rows, the cucumbers laugh,
At cosmic rains and their silly path.
The carrots wiggle, roots in a mess,
As stardust drips, oh what a bless!

So join the fun and wet your feet,
In intergalactic fields so sweet.
With every drip, we're all in sync,
In this wild, watery cosmic link!

Celestial Droppings

Up in the sky, a bird takes flight,
Droppings sparkle, pure delight.
They fall like comets, trail a glow,
Painting the earth with cosmic flow.

With splats of joy on cars and grass,
Aliens giggle as they pass.
Each little plop a starry kiss,
In this universe of whimsical bliss!

Some think it's mess, but oh, you see,
It's a sign from space, a cosmic spree.
Planting laughter, sowing the fun,
In every squish, a star is spun!

So if you see a splash up high,
Just look up and let out a sigh.
For in each droplet, a story's found,
Of laughter echoing all around!

Stardust Stains

Across the ground, a playful trace,
A sprinkle of love from outer space.
With every step, the giggles cling,
In sparkly marks, let laughter ring!

The children chase the shiny marks,
Pretending to catch those little sparks.
In every blot, a wish is made,
For cosmic fun, it won't just fade!

These stains of joy, a vibrant hue,
Each color whispers, "I love you."
They twirl and dance in bright array,
A visible cheer that simply won't sway!

So dance along in the stardust glow,
Embrace the laughter, let it flow.
For every stain tells just one tale,
Of cosmic laughter that'll never pale!

Starry Spoils

In the night sky, something's dropped,
A glittering mess, a mystery plopped.
Aliens giggle, they can't believe,
They scatter the spoils, and take their leave.

With a twinkle and wink, they make a mess,
Leaving behind a royal success.
Starry delights, in every nook,
A treasure trove, just take a look!

Beneath the lamps of distant stars,
Gleaming wonders in paper jars.
A feast for the critters, a banquet out there,
A cosmic spread beyond compare!

So next time you gaze at the twinkling night,
Remember the fun, the sheer delight.
For every star hides a furry tale,
Of the funniest things that make them wail!

Cosmic Fertilizer

In the garden of stars, where dreams take root,
They sprinkle the soil with giggles and hoot.
Worms in the cosmos, they wiggle and writhe,
Mixing the stardust with joy to thrive!

A shower of sparkles, some blue and some green,
Creating a mess that's quite unforeseen.
Planets are laughing, they're rolling around,
As seedlings take flight from the gooey, brown ground!

With every new sprout, a joke's in the air,
Dancing solar flares, with no signs of care.
The sprouts are confetti, the soil is alive,
In this galaxy, happiness thrives!

So grab a shovel, let's dig right in,
With cosmic fertilization, we all can win!
Our laughter will grow, in this wondrous place,
A funny adventure in the vastness of space!

Milky Way Muck

In the Milky Way's depths, what do we find?
A globby delight, of a curious kind.
With a squelch and a splat, it dances about,
A gooey surprise, make no doubt!

Frogs in the stardust, they leap and they sing,
While the muck giggles softly, a marvellous thing.
Planets bounce by, covered in grime,
This cosmic concoction is truly sublime!

So let's splash and play in the mess all around,
With each bubble bursting, laughter is found.
A twirl in the muck, oh, what a delight,
In the cosmic goo, every wrong feels right!

Remember this muck, when stargazing high,
The jolly glop swirling, in the endless sky.
An ode to the fun in the galaxy's wade,
Our laughter's the star that will never fade!

Universal Underdirt

Beneath the surface of vast cosmic lands,
Lies underfoot dirt, we can't understand.
With each tiny crumb, a story unfolds,
Of laughter and mischief in the depths of old!

Galactic critters wiggle with cheer,
Digging for treasures, as we watch near.
They unearth the chuckles, and giggles galore,
As the universe dances, begging for more!

So when you look down at the ground so deep,
Remember the fun that it silently keeps.
Every granule whispers, a jest from the past,
In the underworld's laughter, forever will last!

Let's celebrate this unassuming dirt,
Full of charm, as its tales quietly flirt.
Across the cosmos, under starlit beams,
The playful underdirt fuels our dreams!

Nebula Nourishment

In the depths of space, a feast is found,
Where twinkling stars dance round and round.
With laughter echoing through the sky,
Alien chefs bake pies so high.

Meteorites sprinkle sugar dust,
Filling bellies, it's a must!
Galactic giggles fill the void,
As cosmic cooks get overjoyed.

Planets gather for a grand buffet,
Sampling treats in a zany display.
With every bite, their taste buds cheer,
Floating in joy, they hold their beer.

In banana boats, they glide and glide,
Passing stardust, a slippery ride.
With each delicious, absurd delight,
They munch on joy till the morning light.

Cometary Compost

A comet raced with a tail so bright,
Collecting scraps from its stellar flight.
With leftover lunches from Mars' crew,
It made a mess, oh what to do?

Astronauts laughed with each gooey bit,
Tossing aside what didn't quite fit.
In a cosmic mix, they found delight,
A salad of weirdness, a space-age bite.

The stars all twinkled, full of glee,
Watching their friends munch merrily.
Plans were made for another launch,
For the greatest picnic to ever quench.

As space worms danced upon the ground,
They joined in laughter, a merry sound.
With a wink, the cosmos said, "Why not?"
Let's feast on earthlings' leftovers hot!

Luminous Leftovers

In the dark of night, the light shines through,
Leftovers glimmer, a cosmic stew.
Eager aliens, with forks in hand,
Dive into dishes from a far-off land.

The plates spin round, a galactic show,
Mixing earth spices with asteroids' glow.
"Try this moon pie!" one chef will shout,
As laughter erupts and taste buds sprout.

With every nibble, flavors collide,
A rainbow buffet, oh what a ride!
They toast with stardust, sparkle in their eyes,
Finding joy in the strange and the wise.

Leftovers gleam with an alien twist,
In floating bowls, what's there to resist?
The universe chuckles as they each take a bite,
In this bizarre banquette, everything feels right.

Orbital Offal

Orbiting planets play a prank today,
Flinging offal in a silly way.
With a toss and a giggle, they send it far,
Creating constellations, each a bizarre star.

A piece of pudding from Saturn's moon,
Caught a ride on a rocket, going boom!
While Jupiter laughed and rolled in mirth,
"Who knew that leftovers could have such worth?"

Galactic goop glided through the air,
In a cosmic game, they hadn't a care.
Worms on a comet chirped a sweet song,
While scooping the mess with a gleeful throng.

From the Milky Way, a sweet smell wafted,
As aliens cheered, their laughter grafted.
In the name of fun, they served what they had,
Cosmic chaos, oh this isn't so bad!

Spacetime Straw

In the galaxy's wobbly sway,
Cows float by in a silly ballet.
Their moos echo through the stars,
As they munch on space hay from Mars.

With laser beams instead of grass,
They dine on beams and cosmic sass.
The universe giggles with glee,
As they prance and dance, wild and free.

Gravity's just a gentle joke,
As cows pull pranks, their tails they poke.
Frolicking in the Milky Way,
Making everyone laugh and say,

"Look at those cows, what a sight!
Orbiting around like it's all right."
In the stratosphere, they reign supreme,
Living their best bovine dream!

Supernova Scat

A stellar fart, a burst of glow,
From cows who know how to steal the show.
They leap from stars and give a cheer,
Leaving trails of laughter, oh dear!

Particles dance in the afterflow,
As cows traverse the vast cosmos,
Spreading joy with each cosmic puff,
While the whole universe laughs enough.

Some may call it a cosmic blast,
But it's just cows having a blast.
With giggles echoing through the void,
In their joyful antics, they rejoice.

From nebulae to galaxies wide,
These cows of space take us for a ride.
With each eruption, their spirits soar,
As they dance in stardust forevermore!

Celestial Currents

Riding the waves of the starry stream,
Cows surfing through the universe's dream.
With humor and giggles in each ride,
They spread joy as they glide and slide.

A comet's tail, their favorite slide,
They moo and laugh with cosmic pride.
Orbiting planets, a good old swoop,
Launching themselves in a happy loop.

Through constellations, they weave and dart,
Creating laughter straight from the heart.
Bovine surfing, a ridiculous show,
In the celestial sea, they put on a glow.

In the galaxy's mischievous swirl,
Cows make a splash, giving a twirl.
With giggles resounding, they ride the breeze,
Spreading joy throughout the cosmic seas!

Ethereal Earthy Bits

From the moon to the Milky Way,
Cows scatter joy like it's play day.
With sprinkles of laughter in every bit,
They frolic about, not a care, not a grit.

Their hooves leave footprints in cosmic dust,
Spreading humor is a universal must.
With a twinkle in their starry eyes,
They chuckle at the space-time skies.

Earthy bits fly with each jovial stomp,
As they giggle their way through the cosmic romp.
With every bound in interstellar bliss,
These cheeky cows can't help but twist.

Galactic pranks are all the rage,
In this fun bovine cosmic stage.
With stardust giggles and astral treats,
Cows dance in circles, while laughter repeats!

Astral Alfalfa

In the sky, there's veggie bliss,
Green shoots float with a galactic twist.
Cows in orbit munch with glee,
Spitting seeds for all to see.

Milky Way salads, what a treat,
Salad bowls made of starry wheat.
Laughing cows dance in the mucky prance,
Harvesting hay with a wobbly stance.

Space Hay

From Mars to Pluto, bales are tossed,
Space cows roam, never lost.
Moo-mors in helmets, eating light,
Farmers beam at the silly sight.

Field trips on comets, laughter erupts,
Cows with space suits embracing the fluffs.
Floating farms near supernova glow,
Bale after bale in a cosmic flow.

Cosmic Clusters of Waste

Galactic goo, a grinning pile,
With humor thick, and space-age style.
Meteorites mimic the smelly stacks,
Traces of joy from astral tracks.

Astro-dung, a treasure so bright,
Pushing the stars with all its might.
Aliens chuckle at the spectacle wide,
As fragrant spores on the solar tide.

Interplanetary Poo

Squishy, squashy from out of sight,
Meteor messes bring a giggly bite.
Jupiter's jive, with a splashy plop,
While Saturn's rings start to hop, hop, hop!

Rocket cows leave trails of cheer,
Filling space with fun and beer.
Uranus chuckles at the cosmic crew,
As comets laugh at the smelly stew.

Echoes of the Expanse

In the void where stars do twinkle,
Strange shapes do hurl and crinkle.
Galactic glimmers, some quite round,
Bouncing off from stardust ground.

With laughter reaching light years wide,
Hitchhikers take this cosmic ride.
A dance of joy, what comets throw,
In shimmering paths, they plop like dough.

Wormholes laugh with giddy glee,
As far-off planets look and see.
They wink and giggle, join the play,
In this vast sky, we all stray.

So gather 'round, let echoes ring,
In the expanse, we're all a fling.
With hearty grins and roars we glean,
The universe's wacky scene.

Quantum Grazers

In fields of stars, some creatures munch,
On particles that make a crunch.
They leap through space with joy and cheer,
Nibbling on the cosmic sphere.

Gravitons dance, a tasty treat,
Each bite's a laugh, oh what a feat!
They graze in zero-gravity bliss,
Creating waves, what fun in this!

Quantum quirks in swirling arcs,
Each nibbled snack, a myriad of sparks.
On every whim, they flip and glide,
In playful fields, they dare to ride.

Such cosmic critters, wild and free,
Leave traces of glee for all to see.
Beneath the stars, they twirl and spin,
In this silly game, we all win!

The Milky Way's Mess

Oh what a sight, the stars collide,
In chocolate swirls, where dreams abide.
Sprinkles of light in a creamy flow,
This galaxy's one heck of a show.

Planets roll like marbles tossed,
Through milky rivers, they get lost.
Banana moons and cookie dust,
In this dessert, we laugh, we must.

Sailboats made from candy bars,
Race through the night, beneath the stars.
With each sweet tooth, we float and glide,
In this celestial joyride.

A sprinkle here, a dash of flair,
The mess of worlds, a chaotic fair.
Yet in the chaos, we find delight,
In whimsy's grip, we soar through night.

Lunar Litter

On the moon, what a curious sight,
Trash bins overflow, oh what a fright!
Tinfoil wrappers from snacks galore,
Even a boot that's missed the shore!

Rocket parts left in sheer delight,
Make aliens giggle from sheer height.
With every step on lunar dust,
They point and laugh, oh what a must!

Doritos craters, cosmic spills,
A buffet of snacks on the moon's hills.
With intergalactic party vibe,
Litter bugs dance, it's quite the tribe!

So here's to mess, it's all in fun,
In this moonlit revel, we run and run.
With laughter echoing through the night,
Lunar litter is a sheer delight!

Infinite Intestines

In the depths of the galaxy wide,
Strange droppings take off on a ride.
Twinkling stars giggle with glee,
In the great expanse, who can see?

Galactic cows munching on light,
Digesting space snacks all night.
From their backsides, a comet trail,
Milky Way's finest, they surely prevail.

With every burp and a funky sound,
They scatter joy all around.
Cows from Venus, cows from Mars,
Creating a mess amongst the stars.

So if your spaceship smells a bit,
Just know it's not a cosmic hit.
It's simply the universe's charm,
With funny fragrances galore, no harm!

Marcian Manure

In a far-off realm, where oddballs roam,
A Martian cow has found its home.
With four eyes and a tail so long,
Its daily deeds make the locals strong.

They gather the goo with a chuckle and cheer,
For tractor beams bring it near.
The best fertilizer, the Martians claim,
A cosmic guffaw! What a silly game!

With bubbles afloat and colors so bright,
Droppings of laughter, what a sight!
They sprinkle it down, watch gardens grow,
In the land of red, where fun's all aglow.

Just watch your step on the lunar tiles,
Where Marcian manure brings endless smiles.
In the heart of space, no need to pout,
When alien poop is what it's about!

Cosmic Contributions

From black holes come odd little gifts,
Droppings of joy that time shifts.
Asteroids roll with a whiff and a wink,
In the flow of the universe, they stink!

Contributors to the intergalactic soil,
With a laugh, those strange beings toil.
They trade their treasures for silly delight,
Stardust and giggles light up the night.

When Saturnian rings start to sparkle and shine,
You'll spot something funny, just give it time.
A cosmic offering, a giggly gift,
That keeps on giving, gives the mood a lift.

So thank the stars for their quirky ways,
For the joy they bring on mundane days.
Every pile that's dropped, a tale on its own,
In the universe's laughter, we're never alone!

Planetary Piles

On a distant world, known for its fun,
Cows roam free beneath two suns.
They prance and jump, without a care,
Leaving their mark in the alien air.

With every step, a giggle erupts,
As planets collect their quirky corrupts.
Jupiter grins while Venus snorts,
Creating piles of interstellar sorts.

Green grass grows from these quirky heaps,
Where aliens frolic and laughter leaps.
From Martian fields to Saturn's rings,
A cosmic ballet of amusing things.

So if you ever fly through space,
Remember the joy and the silly grace.
For in each planet's playful defile,
Lies a universe brimming with smiles!

Celestial Fertilizer

In the vastness of space, oh what a sight,
Planets trotting, both day and night.
With their droppings gleaming, a sparkly show,
They sprinkle the cosmos, where no one would go.

Alien cows munching on stardusty grass,
Leaving behind treasures, oh what a class!
Astronauts chuckle and roll in the goo,
Making space suits their new fancy brew.

Meteorite muffins, they fly with delight,
Orbiting laughter, oh what a flight!
Galactic wisecracks, from stars up above,
Whispering jokes that all creatures would love.

In the expanse, there's no place too far,
Where fun finds a way near each glittering star.
So laugh with the tides of the moon's gentle sway,
At the cosmic creations that brightened the day.

Nebula Nuggets

Floating in space, what a bizarre feast,
Nuggets of nonsense, to say the least!
Comets zoom by, with a wacky delight,
As laughter erupts in the endless night.

Galactic chickens from planets unknown,
Lay eggs of starlight, from cosmic they've grown.
Bubbles of chuckles that dance in the void,
Creating a symphony that can't be destroyed.

Asteroids tumble, they bump and they roll,
Like a game of marbles, with laughter their goal.
In the cradle of space, where humor is free,
They gather their nuggets, for all to see.

So twinkle, dear stars, in your playful embrace,
For joy in the cosmos is a curious chase.
From this silly corner of the vast, endless sea,
We chuckle at nuggets, between you and me.

Astral Hay Bales

In pastures of space, where comets roam,
Hay bales are scattered, they're finding a home.
Shooting stars giggle, as they tumble in piles,
Creating a ruckus with comical smiles.

Interstellar farmers, with hats made of light,
Harvesting laughter throughout the night.
Plucking the hay from the milky way's dome,
They stack up the fun, in a nebula home.

Round bales of mirth, they roll down the plains,
Leaving trails of joy, like sweet candy canes.
A barn full of whimsy, under the sun,
Where celestial critters all gather for fun.

So dance in the stardust, take joy in the ride,
As cowboys of cosmos wear laughter with pride.
With hay bales a-plenty, and smiles at their side,
In this funny universe, no need to hide.

Starlit Scat

Twinkling so brightly, the stars take a lead,
With little star droppings, comedy's seed.
They sparkle and shimmer, what a funny sight,
As the universe chuckles in endless delight.

Furry creatures bouncing on beams of pure light,
Leave behind scat that's a humorous fright.
Like stardust confetti, they dance through the skies,
Creating outbursts of laughter and sighs.

Meteors pry for a comedic reprieve,
Trailing behind them, backups they leave.
Jokes that are cosmic, are best by the moon,
In the theater of dreams, we chuckle in tune.

So let us rejoice in the funny and grand,
As starlit shenanigans come close at hand.
With laughter our guide through the heavens afar,
We chase after joy in this dance with a star.

Galactic Pastures

In fields of stars where cows do roam,
They munch on stardust, far from home.
They laugh and moo in zero-grav,
Leaving trails of giggles, oh what a salve!

With milk that tastes like comet's cream,
They churn the laughter, a cosmic dream.
The farmers dance in moonlight glow,
Scooping dreams from the space below.

Galaxies spin with joyous glee,
As cows frolic, wild and free.
From black holes that suck away the night,
Comes a chorus of hooves, a funny sight!

So if you wander through this vast spree,
Watch your step, it's hard to see.
For in these pastures of sky and fun,
You might just find a starry bun!

Starry Droppings

The night is bright with twinkling eyes,
As cows drop gems from the cosmic skies.
Sparkling bits of laughter and light,
Decorating fields in the chilly night.

Each little plop's a cosmic joke,
Rolling softly, like stardust smoke.
Farmers chuckle, with shovels in hand,
Collecting treasures from the space-land.

They toss them high for the sun to greet,
Creating craters where cows skipped their feet.
And all the critters, they dance around,
In a festival of fun on stardust ground!

So watch your step in the milky haze,
For starry droppings set the world ablaze.
With laughter echoing across the field,
The joys of the night are brightly revealed!

Moonlit Meadows

In meadows bathed in lunar light,
The cows convene, a comical sight.
They prance and jump, under the glow,
Leaving a trail of giggles to sow.

Their bellies full of meteor pies,
They chuckle loudly, oh what a prize!
With frolicsome hooves and starry tunes,
They dance away in the light of moons.

Each little fart sends sparkles high,
Making rainbows swirl across the sky.
Cows jump and twirl in silly delight,
Painting the night with laughter so bright!

So if you wander by moonlit streams,
Join in the fun with laughter and dreams.
For in these meadows where cows let loose,
Even the stars roll with the produce!

Interstellar Manure

In the depths of space, a surprise they found,
Bovine treasures scattered 'round.
A legacy of laughter in countless heaps,
As farmers chuckle while space-sheep bleat!

From planets far and wide they came,
Delivering joy in a funny game.
With every scoop, a tale to tell,
Of intergalactic fun they know so well.

Astro-cows with their cosmic trot,
Leave behind a giggly plot.
And with each pile, a story unfolds,
Of moonlit mischief, and laughter bold.

So grab a shovel, come join the fun,
In this universe where gags are spun.
For even in space, if you take a chance,
You'll find joy, laughter, and a silly dance!

www.ingramcontent.com/pod-product-compliance
Lightning Source LLC
Chambersburg PA
CBHW051701160426
43209CB00004B/977